THIS BOOK BELONGS TO

HI THERE I'M GOING TO TEACH YOU WHAT THE WEATHER IS LIKE.

What do you see through the window?

Sun. When we can see the Sun, we say it's sunny.
SUNNY

SUNNY
SUNNY
SUNNY
SUNNY
SUNNY

What do you see through the window?

Oh, there are clouds. When we see many clouds in the sky we say it's cloudy.
CLOUDY

CLOUDY
CLOUDY
CLOUDY
CLOUDY

What do you see through the window?

The rain. when there are clouds droplets fall down and we say it's raining.
RAINY

RAINY
RAINY
RAINY
RAINY

What do you see through the window?

Whoa it's thunder and lightning. When we see thunder and see lightning coming out of the clouds, we say there's a storm. Thunderstorms forms only when very very cold air and worm air meets in the sky.
 STORMY

STORMY
STORMY
STORMY
STORMY

What do you see now?

Whoa there's snowfall. when it's cold and snowflakes fall from the sky, we say it's snowing.
When rain drops freezes and turns into snow at $0^0$ Degree Celsius ($32^0$ F).
SNOWY

SNOWY
SNOWY
SNOWY
SNOWY

What do you see through the window?

Trees are moving and the wind is blowing heavily. When you see things moving or flying around in the street that's because it's windy.
WINDY

WINDY

WINDY

WINDY

WINDY

WINDY

# weather icons

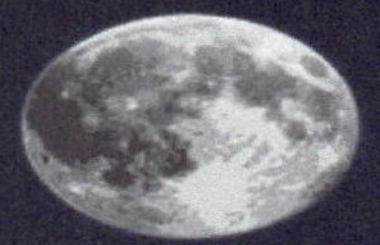

Full moon

Half moon

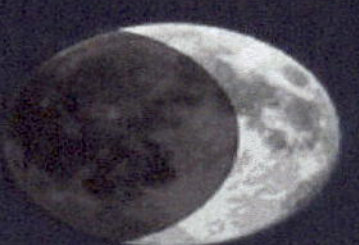

Crescent

New moon

Sunny

Sunny to cloudy

Cloudy

Overcast

Sun rain

Showers

Heavy rain

Snowy

Thunder

Fog

Frost

Windy

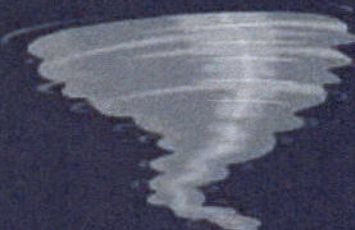

Stormy

Cold

Warm

Hot

Weather and climate are not the same. The key difference between them is time. Climate is the average weather of a region for a long period of time, usually about 30 years. Weather on the other hand is constantly changing from hour to hour, minute to minute and second to second.

TOOLS USED TO MEASURE WEATHER.
Weather instruments are tools that meteorologists use to measure weather. Measuring weather helps people plan what to wear and lets people know if they need to carry an umbrella. it also helps meteorologists find weather patterns and predict future weather.

TEMPERATURE- THERMOMETER
when measuring temperature, we use thermometers to measure degrees, the red line in the middle of the thermometer moves up and down. if you look closely there are two sets of numbers one is for Fahrenheit, the other is for Celsius. in the United States we measure temperature using Fahrenheit. make sure you look for the letter F when you are measuring temperature.

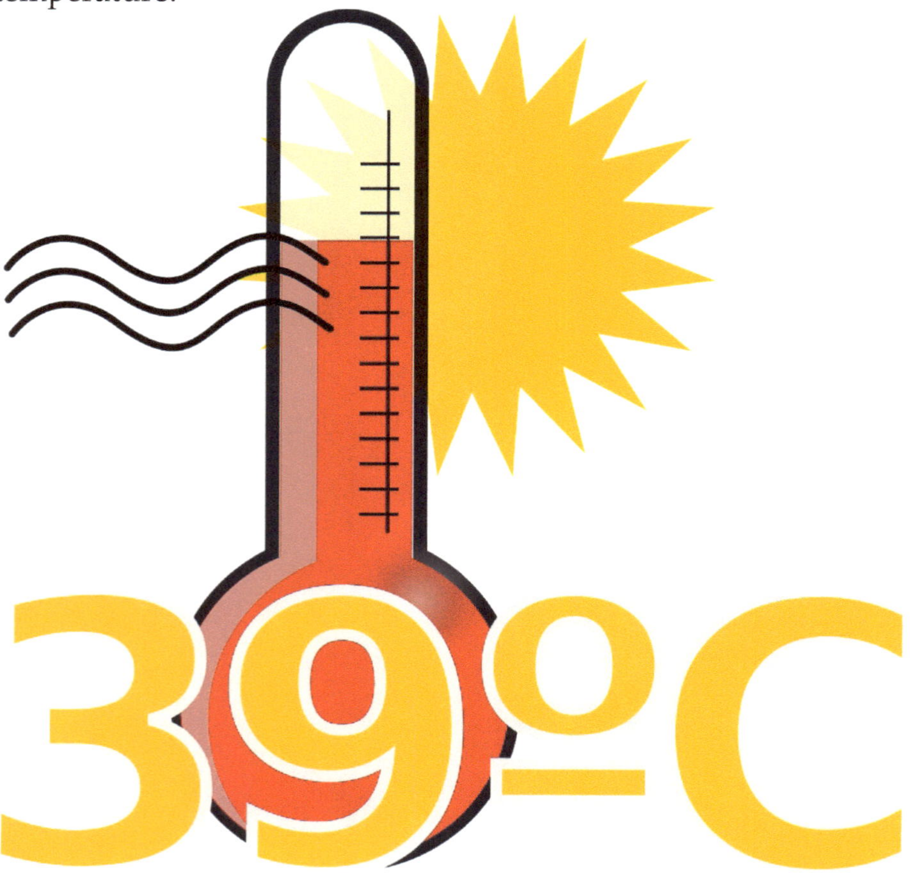

# RAIN- RAIN GAUGE

 a rain gauge measures rainfall. a gauge is a clear container with straight sides it is marks for inches or centimeters on the side. as rain falls it fills up the gauge and can be measured.

# SNOWFALL- RULER

 measuring snowfall is easy. before it snows, put a board on a flat ground outdoors. when it stops snowing put a ruler into the snow until it touches the board, and measure how high is the snow.

# WIND- WIND VANE

wind vane or a wind sock measures the wind direction. an anemometer catches the wind in spinning cups to measure its speed.

# SEASONS

Dear children we shall learn the names of season

# SUMMER

It is very hot and in summer we wear cotton clothes, eat cold ice cream and drink cold drinks.
Summer is a vacation season.

# WINTER

Winters are very cold and chilly. Snows falls in winter season.
We wear warm woolen clothes in winter. the foods liked in this time are hot foods and drinks like tea coffee etc.

# SPRING

Spring is a pleasant, warm and picnic season. it comes with the blossoming of colorful flowers.

# AUTUMN

Autumn is the season when the trees shed their leaves. the climate is pleasant.

# RAINY SEASON

 The coming of monsoons bring the rainy season. people are seen with colorful umbrellas and raincoats. we like to eat plenty of fried food in the rainy season. Rain is essential for proper growth of crops.

USE YOUR WEATHER KNOWLEDGE TO DECIDE WHICH SEASON THEY ARE IN AND
WRITE THE APROPRITE SEASON NAME BELOW THE IMAGES.

# RAINBOW

can you tell me all the colors in the rainbow?
Violet, indigo, blue, green, yellow, orange and red.
VIBGYOR
that's the way to remember it.

All seven colors and it looks so pretty. But how is a rainbow formed? Rainbows are spectacular.

Rays of sunlight looks white, but it's really made of different colors. A rainbow is seen when the Sun shines after the rain. White light is made of seven colors.
Wow what's this?
Let me explain it to you with the help of the prism. The Sun forms a rainbow when white light passes through raindrops. The raindrops act like tiny prisms. When sunlight passes through a raindrop it bends and scatters into the band of colors. This can be reflected back to you as a rainbow.

But where do I look for a rainbow?

You need to remember three things.
FIRST - It must be raining it must be raining.
SECOND -the Sun must be shining.
THIRD- you must be between the Sun
and the rain.
Okay. Now let's enjoy watching the wonderful rainbow.

# OUR PLANET, EARTH

Earth is the blue planet; Earth is the planet where we live. Earth is the 3rd planet from the sun. 29% of Earth's surface is land and the remaining 71% is covered with water. Earth is the 5th largest planet in the solar system. Earth revolves around the Sun. Earth takes 365 days to Complete a one circle around sun. And Earth has only one satellite Moon. The Moon revolves around earth.

# EARTH CONTINENTS

There are 7 continents on the Earth.
7 Continents are Asia, Europe, North America, South America, Africa, Australia, Antarctica.

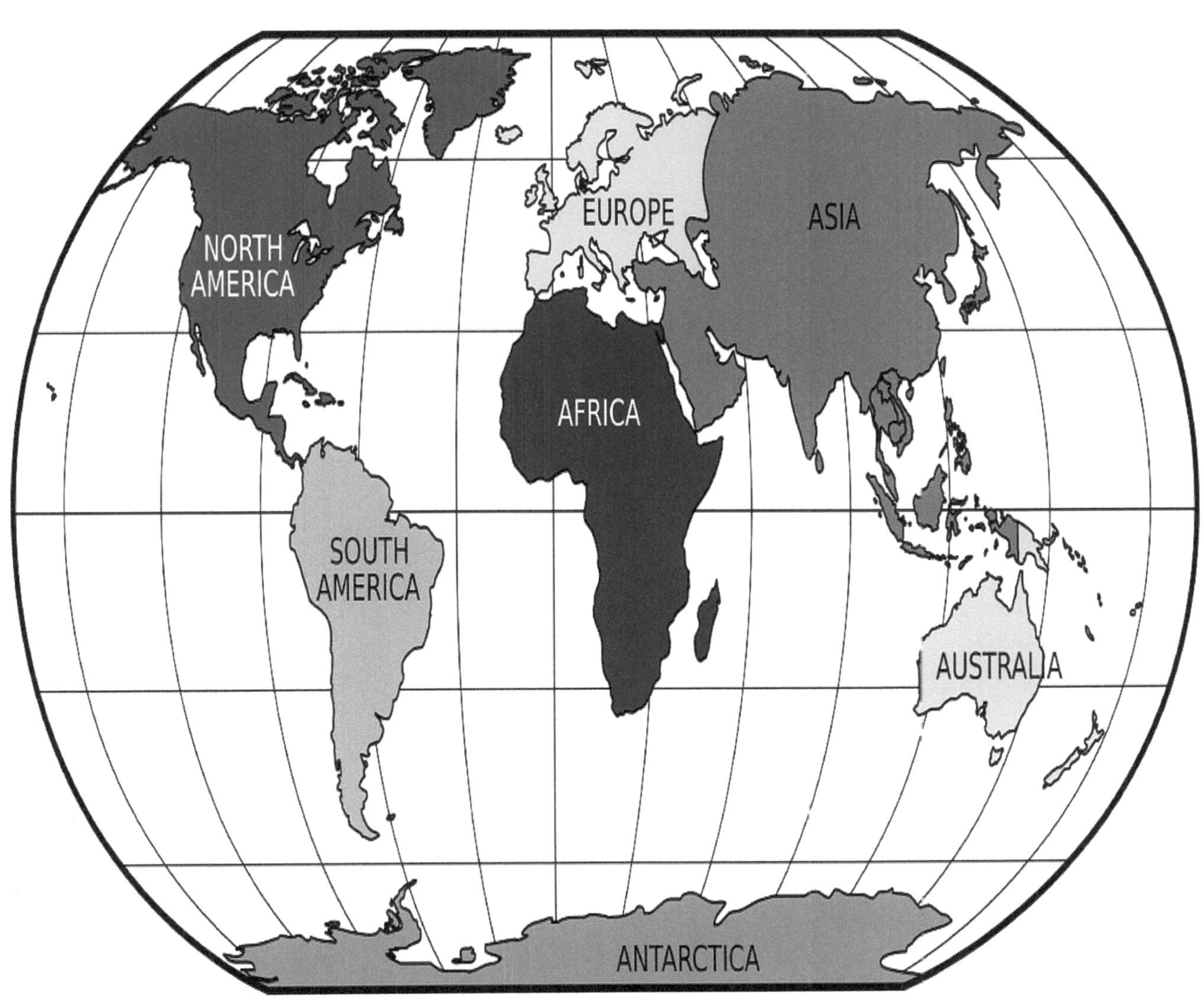

# OCEANS

There are 7 oceans on the Earth. They are **Arctic**, North **Atlantic**, South **Atlantic**, **North Pacific**, South Pacific, **Indian**, and Southern Oceans.

# COUNTRIES

There are about 200 countries on the Earth.

There are over 7 billion people on the Earth.
There are various animals and plants on the Earth.

# WATER CYCLE

Hey! Have you ever wondered where the rain comes from?" Or how the clouds are formed? Well, this is what the water cycle is all about. Come let's explore!

When the sun heats up the rivers and oceans, water becomes water vapour and it rises up in the air. This process is called **evaporation**. It is the first step of the water cycle.
You too can see water vapour at home! Just tell your mommy to heat some water. And as the water gets heated, you'll be able to see the water vapour rising up in the air.

When the water vapour reaches up in the sky, it turns into tiny droplets of water. These water droplets along with various gases and dust particles, come together to form clouds. This is known as **condensation**.

Now, hold a cold lid over the vessel in which you heated water. When you open the lid after sometime, you'll be able to see water droplets on the lid. That's exactly what condensation is!

When the cloud becomes too heavy and it cannot hold any more water inside, it bursts open to give out rain, hail or snow. This is known as **precipitation**.

As it rains, water gets collected in oceans, lakes and rivers. It even seeps through the soil and becomes ground water. Thus water cycle is a continuous process of evaporation, condensation and precipitation.

Did you know that even plants sweat? That's called **transpiration**. That's why it rains more in places with more trees, like hill stations and forests.

Sometimes snow directly turns into water vapour without melting into water. That's called **sublimation**. This happens a lot in cold countries.

# SOLAR SYSTEM

There are Mercury, Venus, Earth, Mars, Jupiter, Saturn, Uranus, and Neptune. They go around the Sun. This is our Solar System.

# SUN

The Sun is very big and hot.

## MERCURY

Mercury is the closest planet to the Sun.

## VENUS

Venus is the brightest planet in the sky.

## EARTH

Earth is our planet.

## MARS

Mars is a red planet.

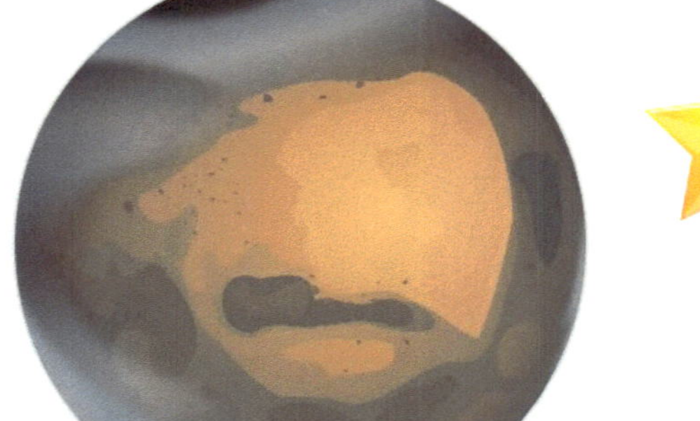

## JUPITER

Jupiter is the largest planet.

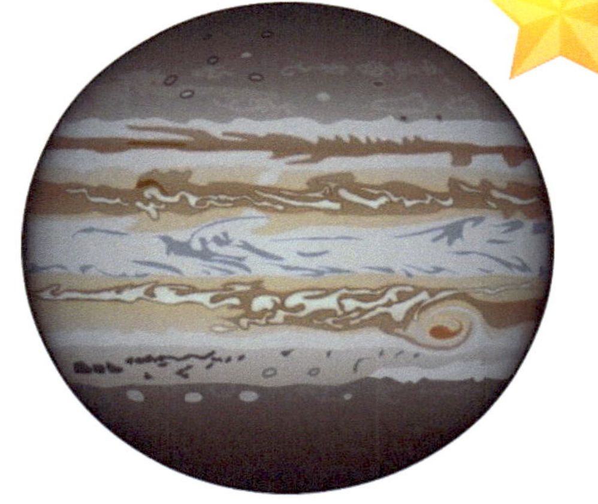

## SATURN

Saturn is the planet with the rings.

## URANUS

Uranus is very cold and cloudy.

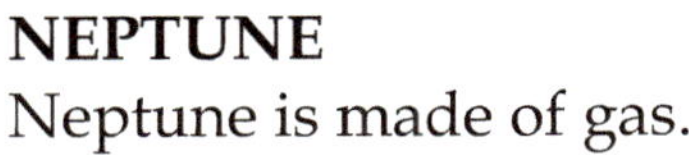

## NEPTUNE

Neptune is made of gas.

# PHOTOSYNTHESIS

Yes you're right Mr. Tree! Isn't the process called Photosynthesis? Yeah. Come friends, let's learn about Photosynthesis today. I'll tell you what it means. 'Photo' means Light and 'Synthesis' means 'Putting together'. Now, it's simple! Photosynthesis is using light to put things together! Plants use this process to make their food with the help of sunlight, water and carbon dioxide.

CO2
C6H12O6
O2
H2O
H2O
H2O

Did you know that plants breathe just like us? You didn't? Well, now you do! Plants have tiny openings called the Stomata, present in their leaves, through which they take in carbon dioxide. Yes, they breathe in carbon dioxide and give out oxygen. They also use water and other nutrients to make food which is absorbed by their roots. The leaves contain tiny pigments called the Chloroplasts. These pigments take in carbon dioxide, water and sunlight, and turn them into sugar and oxygen. The sugar is then used by the plants as their food, and the oxygen is given out into the atmosphere This process as a whole is called "Photosynthesis."

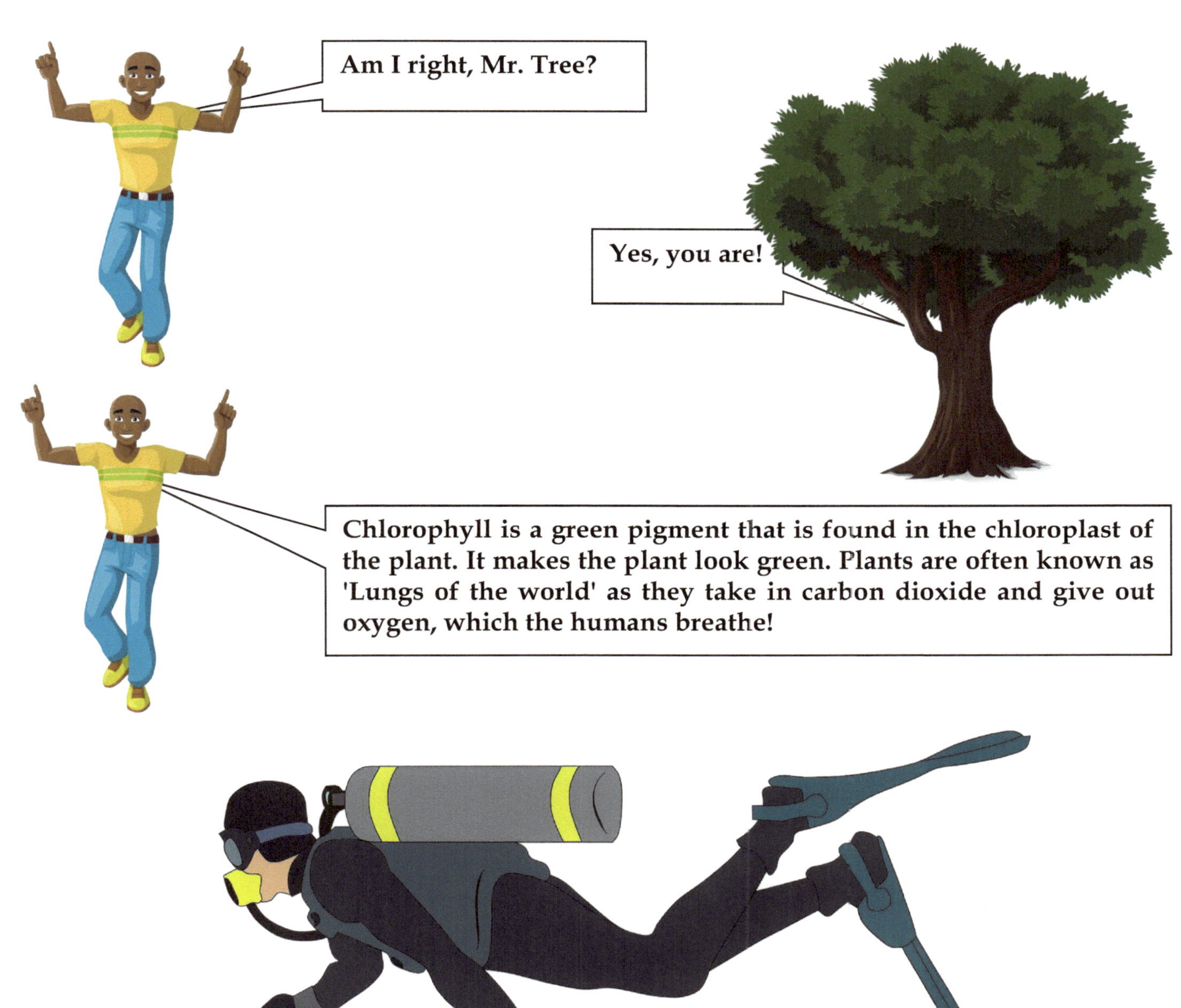

Am I right, Mr. Tree?
Yes, you are!
Chlorophyll is a green pigment that is found in the chloroplast of the plant. It makes the plant look green. Plants are often known as 'Lungs of the world' as they take in carbon dioxide and give out oxygen, which the humans breathe!

Thank you for reading this book.
If you liked this book, please share the link of this book with your friends and family, classmates and let them buy this book and Help them to get more knowledge about Weather and Nature.